#

Coded Coloring Pages for KIDS of All Ages

Vol. 2

Lorraine Holnback Brodek

GRIDDLES:
Coded Coloring Pages for KIDS of All Ages
Vol. 2

Contact Lorraine Holnback Brodek at www.LorraineBrodek.com

Cover Design – June Holzwarth, who can be contacted through
LinkedIn.com or at (203) 385-3432

Editing and Formatting – Donna Hawkins, donnadelayed@hotmail.com

Published by Lorraine Holnback Brodek
Printed by CreateSpace, an Amazon.com Company
ISBN-13: 978-1522939573 / ISBN-10: 1522939571

Dedication

A lot more goes into designing a coloring book than meets the eye. Big THANK YOU's to:

My two sanity coaches who translated my grid designs into computer-speak:

Donna Hawkins, whose editing and formatting skills are the best. Her "atta-girl's" kept me from flipping (the page, that is).

June Holzwarth, who created a great title, then filled the cover with color and fun! Speaking of pages, she also was on the same page as my grandson...

Logan Dunn, who said, "Grandma, what you really should do is write a clue for each picture. Kids love that!" He's 14. He knows everything.

Jo, who tested my designs while her cute doggie, Violet, helped sharpen her pencils.

Marianne, who kept me in the zone even though she wasn't, and said, "I am WAY not a grid person, but all the kids are going to love these! So cute!"

Then...husband, Tom, who claimed, "I'd like to help code designs, but I have to go play pasture golf. However, when I get home I can help you scan."

Last, but always first, daughters Kristin and Kerri who, when asked what their mother does, answer, "She's an air traffic controller."

A LITTLE INTRODUCTION

WHY: One theory has it that the left side of the brain controls logic, accuracy, and math, while the right side controls creativity, color, and visual skills. Let's just say this coloring book will stimulate both sides of your brain, with the purpose of fun and focus, along with a dose of decoding designs. Each page is a puzzle and an art project all in one. This mental exercise can be mesmerizing, as you become engrossed in watching the grid picture evolve by following the color code.

WHAT MADE ME DO IT: Back in the 1970s, my step-mom, Betty, and I started a needlecraft company called *Fingerworks*, where we produced kits with small cross stitch and needlepoint designs that were named *Fingerprints* because they were...little prints. Through the years, friends have asked me to convert my whimsical designs into a book. So, I have finally decided to do my part to help stimulate our brains and keep our noggins from foggin'.

WHAT'S INSIDE: The grids in this book are 3 squares per inch. This will provide fun for kids of all ages, with some of the easier designs using fewer colors. You'll be able to determine this by looking at the code first.

Since we sometimes lose track of our lines, I've added a guide for that. There is an "L"-shaped Line Guide template on page 95. You can cut, then trace or paste it onto heavy paper. Cut out this thicker template and use it as your line guide. Or, you can use an L-Square Ruler (by Westcott). There are also blank graphs in the back, in case you want to redo designs with your own color choices or make cleaner copies. You can also create some artwork of your own.

But wait . . . there's more – I've also included black and white solutions to each puzzle in the back of the book, but try not to peek!

STUFF YOU'LL NEED: Crayons work well on these larger grids. I love all the colors that Crayola has now (plus their fun names), as well as their markers. Colored pencils are great too, and Crayola offers a line called *Twistables* that are terrific. Prismacolor has good color selections in both its *Soft Core* and *Verithin* versions. Also, I've found that by using pink-capped pencil eraser tops (Paper Mate, Staples), I can actually erase some of my mistakes. Gel pens (Fiskars Classroom Set) and fine-tipped markers provide good coverage.

HINTS: To prevent mistakes, just put a dot of color in each square that is listed in the code. If the color you're using is "Red" and the code says: "12: C,D" just put a dot of red in each of those squares. You can then go back and fill in when you've completed your design. There are blank pages between designs to prevent ink from penetrating through (if gel pens are your choice). You can also use these pages to test colors that you might want to use for the next design. To soften the robotic look of chart art, you can outline the components of your artwork with a thin-tipped pencil or pen.

FOR STITCHERY FANS: Any of these designs can be converted to cross stitch, needlepoint or some quilting projects, as these crafts are based on grid patterns. Each square represents one X-shaped color that will form a picture in a raster-like pattern. Digital imaging is also based on this system, where photo images are formed by pixels per inch (PPI) or dots per inch (DPI). So, this is like an introduction to Computer Graphics #101!

MANY THANKS FOR PUTTING MY CHART ART IN YOUR HANDCART!

I HOPE YOU HAVE AS MUCH FUN COUNTING AND COLORING AS I DID.

Clue: Got milk?

BLACK
5: H,I,J,K,L,M,N
6: G,H,I,J,L,M,N,O
7: B,C,D,E,F,G,H,I,J,L,M,N,O,P,Q,R,S,T
8: A,E,F,G,H,N,O,P,Q,U
9: A,B,C,D,F,G,H,N,O,P,R,S,T,U
10: G,H,N,O
11: F,G,H,I,J,K,L,M,N,O,P
12: E,F,G,H,I,J,K,L,M,N,O,P,Q
13: E,F,G,H,I,J,K,L,M,N,O,P,Q
14: E,F,K,P,Q
15: E,Q
16: I,M
17: H,I,J,L,M,N
18: I,M

BRIGHT PINK
8: B,C,D,R,S,T
14: G,H,I,J,L,M,N,O
15: F,G,H,I,J,K,L,M,N,O,P
16: E,F,G,K,O,P,Q
17: E,F,G,K,O,P,Q
18: E,F,G,K,O,P,Q
19: E,F,G,H,I,J,K,L,M,N,O,P,Q
20: F,G,H,I,M,N,O,P

MEDIUM BROWN
3: G,O
4: G,H,N,O
5: G,O

BLACK
Make circles:
9: J and L

BLACK LINES
1. For fun, make 3 vertical short lines at angles coming out of the center top of her head for tufts of hair.
2. Outline both nostrils with black circles, then fill in with color to lines.

GREEN LINES
If you want her to be eating grass, make about 4 horizontal lines at angles coming out of either side of her mouth.

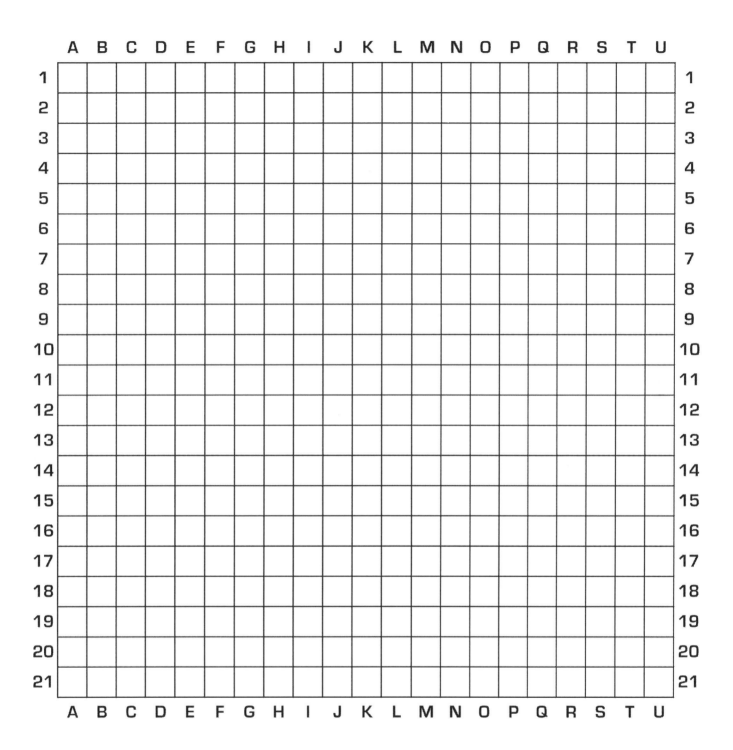

GRID 2

Clue: Cousin of Hamm from "Toy Story."

PINK
5: G,H,I,J,K,L,M
6: E,F,L,M,N,O
7: D,E,F,G,H,I,J,K,L,M,N,O,P
8: C,D,E,F,G,H,J,K,P
9: C,D,E,F,G,K,L,M,Q,R
10: C,D,E,F,G,H,J,K,L,M,O,P,Q,R
11: C,D,E,F,G,H,J,K,L,M,N,O,P,Q,R,S
12: C,D,E,F,H,J,L,M,N,O,P,Q,R
13: D,E,F,G,K,L,M,N,O,P,Q,R
14: D,E,F,G,H,J,K,L,M,N,O,P,Q
15: E,F,G,H,J,K,L,M,N,O,P
16: F,G,H,I,J,K,L,M,N,O
17: F,G,H,M,N,O
18: G,N,O

DARK PINK
5: P,Q,R
6: B,G,H,I,J,K,P,Q,R
7: A,Q
8: A,B,L,M,N,O
9: B,N,O
10: N,S,T
11: T
12: S
15: Q
16: P,Q

GOLDEN YELLOW
8: I
9: H,J
10: I

ORANGE
Make a solid circle:
9: I

GREEN
11: I
12: G,I,K
13: H,I,J
14: I
15: I

BLACK
Make solid circles:
8: Q
9: P
Draw a circle outline to make a ring between 10 and 11 in column "U."

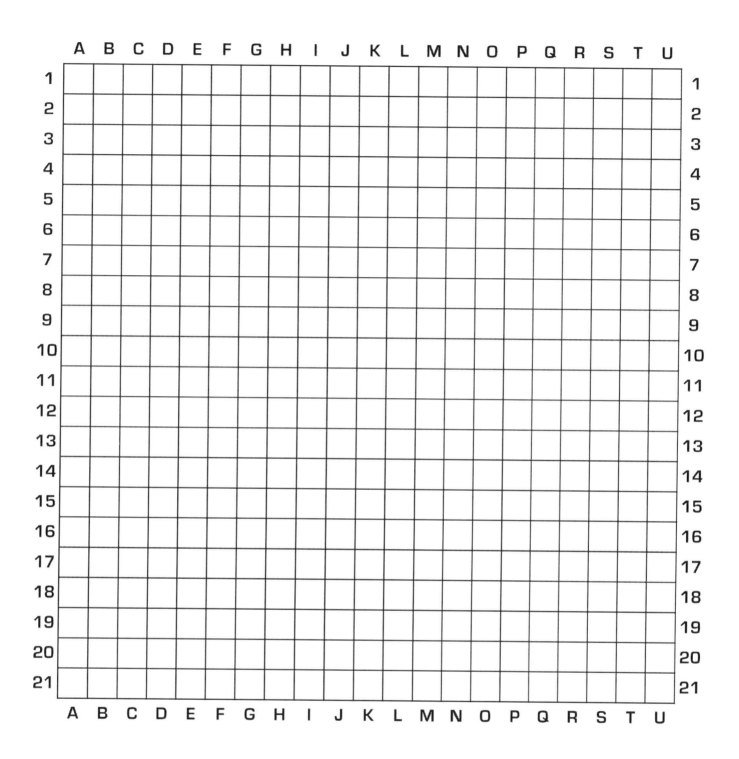

GRID 3

Clue: A fly-by-night job.

DARK GREEN
12: D,E,F,O,P,Q
13: C,D,F,O,Q,R
14: C,D,E,P,Q,R
15: C,E,P,R
16: C,D,Q,R
17: C,D,E,P,Q,R
18: D,E,F,O,P,Q
19: F,G,N,O
20: D,E,F,G,N,O,P,Q

BLACK
Draw a thick black line for smile:
From lower left corner: 8: H
Across to lower left corner: 8: I
Down to lower left corner: 9: I
Diagonal line to lower right: 10: I
Across to lower left corner: 10: L
Diagonal line to lower right: 9: L
Up to lower right corner: 8: L
Across to lower right corner: 8: M

MEDIUM GREEN
5: G,H,M,N
6: F,I,L,O
7: F,I,J,K,L,O
8: G,H,I,J,K,L,M,N
9: G,H,I,J,K,L,M,N
10: G,I,J,K,L,N
11: H,M
12: I,L
13: G,H,M,N
14: F,G,N,O
15: F,G,N,O
16: F,G,N,O
17: F,G,N,O
18: G,H,M,N
19: H,I,L,M
20: H,I,L,M

BLACK
Make solid circles:
6: H,N (in upper right
corners)

LIGHT GREEN
10: H,M
11: I,J,K,L
12: J,K
13: E,I,J,K,L,P
14: H,I,J,K,L,M
15: D,H,I,J,K,L,M,Q
16: E,H,I,J,K,L,M,P
17: H,I,J,K,L,M
18: I,J,K,L
19: J,K

BLACK
Make solid circles:
2: S
3: R
Starting from the center
where black circles meet,
draw two small loops to fill
each square for wings:
2: R
3: S

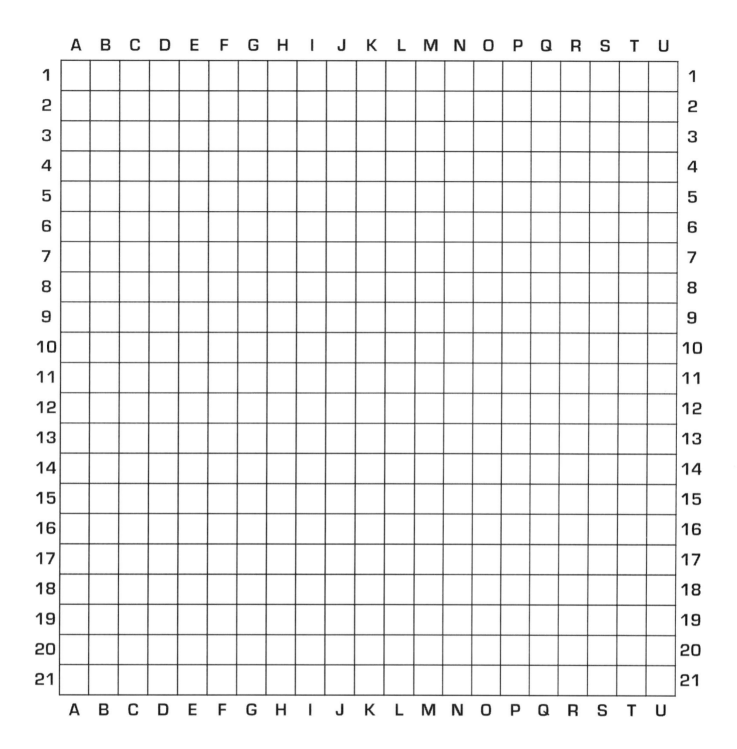

Clue: His unknown brother, Grumpo, wore these.

BLACK
2: C,E,G,H,O,P,R,T
3: C,D,E,F,G,H,O,P,Q,R,S,T
4: C,D,E,F,G,H,I,N,O,P,Q,R,S,T
5: C,J,M,T
6: D,E,F,G,H,I,N,O,P,Q,R,S
7: C,D,J,K,L,M,S,T
8: C,D,J,K,L,M,S,T
9: D,J,M,S
10: D,J,M,S
11: E,I,N,R
12: F,G,H,O,P,Q
17: G,H,I,N,O,P
18: F,G,H,I,J,K,L,M,N,O,P,Q
19: G,H,I,J,K,L,M,N,O,P
20: H,J,L,N

PINK
9: K,L
10: K,L
11: J,K,L,M
12: I,J,K,L,M,N
13: I,J,K,L,M,N
14: H,I,J,K,L,M,N,O
15: G,H,I,J,K,L,M,N,O,P
16: G,H,I,J,K,L,M,N,O,P
17: J,K,L,M

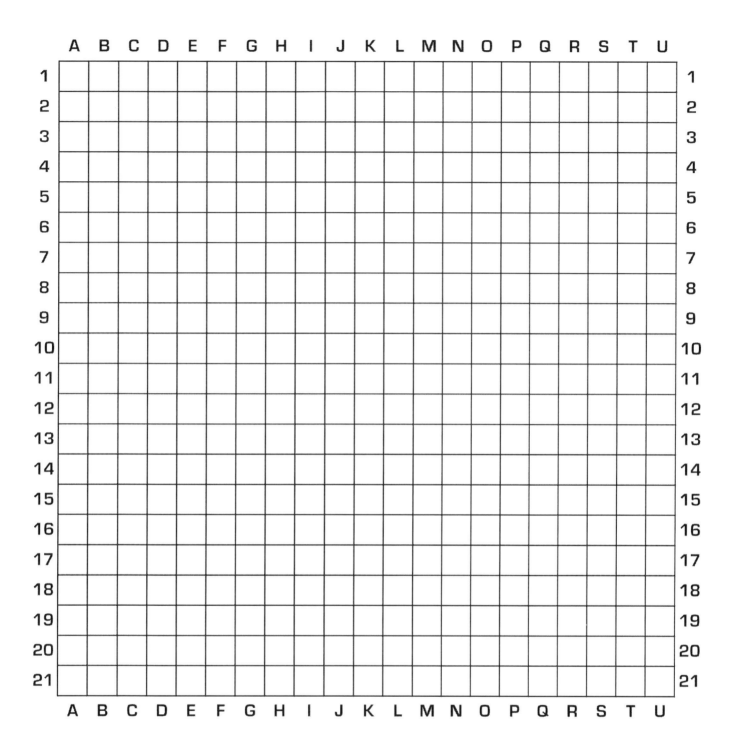

GRID 5

Clue: Smarter than the average.

MEDIUM or GOLDEN BROWN
4: I,J,Q,R
5: H,K,L,M,N,O,P,S
6: H,J,K,L,M,N,O,P,Q,S
7: I,J,K,L,M,N,O,P,Q,R
8: I,J,K,L,M,N,O,P,Q,R
9: I,J,K,M,N,P,Q,R
10: I,J,K,L,O,P,Q,R
11: J,K,L,O,P,Q
12: H,K,L,O,P,S
13: H,I,J,Q,R,S
14: H,I,J,K,M,N,P,Q,R,S
15: G,H,I,J,K,L,M,N,O,P,Q,R,S,T
16: J,K,L,M,N,O,P,Q
17: I,L,M,N,O,R
18: H,M,N,S
19: H,M,N,S
20: I,L,O,R
21: J,K,P,Q

PINK
5: I,J,Q,R
6: I,R
12: G,T
13: F,G,T,U
14: F,G,T,U
17: J,K,P,Q
18: I,J,K,L,O,P,Q,R
19: I,J,K,L,O,P,Q,R
20: J,K,P,Q

TURQUOISE BLUE
1: C,D,E,F
2: B,C,D,E,F,G
3: B,C,D,E,F,G
4: B,C,D,E,F,G
5: C,D,E,F
6: D,E
7: D,E
13: K,L,M,N,O,P
14: L,O

BLACK
Make circles:
9: L and O

BLACK LINE
For string, draw line across at lower:
6: D through F
Curve line down from lower left 6:D
Down middle of row C: 7,8,9,10, 11
Curve line back to paw at 13: F
Start line again at 14: F and curve down to 17: E

BLACK "V"
Make a capital "V" to fill each square for smile:
11: M and N

BLACK CIRCLE
Make a larger round dot for nose where 2 "V's" meet: at intersection of 10 and 11 and M and N.

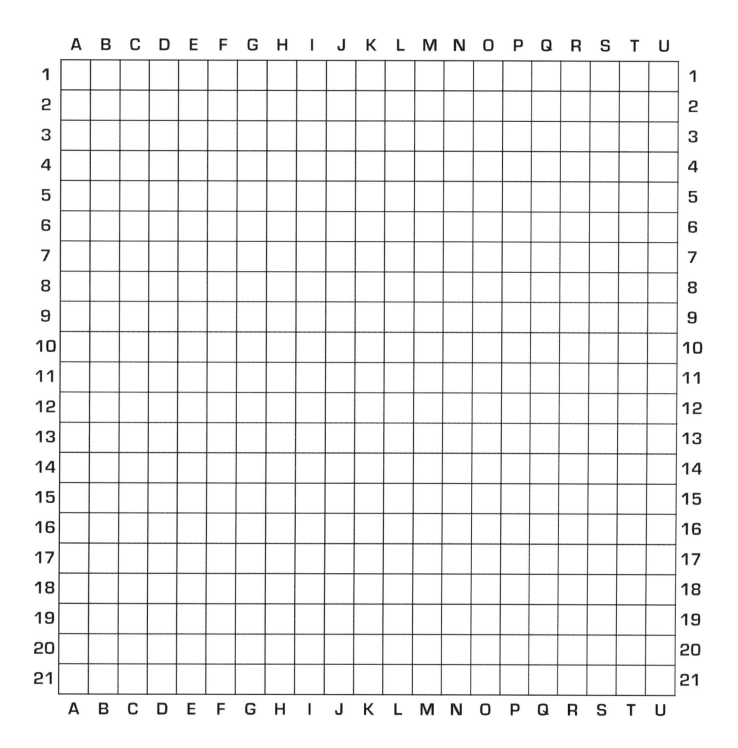

Clue: Though blue, she only sings happy songs.

DARK PINK
10: M,R
11: M,N,Q,R
12: M,N,O,P,Q
13: L,M,N,O,P,Q
14: K,L,M,N,O,P

MEDIUM BROWN
14: T
15: S
16: G,H,I,J,K,L,M,N,O,P,Q,R
17: F
18: D,E

GREEN
16: D,S
17: E,H,I,J
18: I
19: K

LIGHT GREEN
15: D
16: E
17: T
18: J,K

LIGHT TURQUOISE
3: N,O,P,Q
4: E,M,N,O,P,Q,R
5: E,F,L,M,N,R,S
6: C,D,E,F,G,L,M,S
7: G,H,L,M,S
8: H,I
9: I,J,K,L,M,N,R,S
10: E,F,G,H,I,J,K,N,O,P,Q,S
11: F,G,H,I,J,K,O,P,S
12: G,H,I,J,R
13: R
14: Q
15: J,K,L,M,N,O,P

TURQUOISE
7: F,I,J,K
8: G,J,K,L
9: H
10: D,L
11: E,L
12: F,K,L
13: G,H,I,J,K
14: H,I,J
Make a solid round blue circle:
7: O

BLACK
Draw a left arrowhead (<) to fill square:
8: M

Draw a curved line at bottom of line:
8: N and O
Connect this line to bottom of left arrowhead in 8: M.

Draw a curved diagonal line from upper left corner down to lower right corner for feet:
16: M and O

GOLDEN YELLOW
Fill in left arrowhead (<) at:
8: M

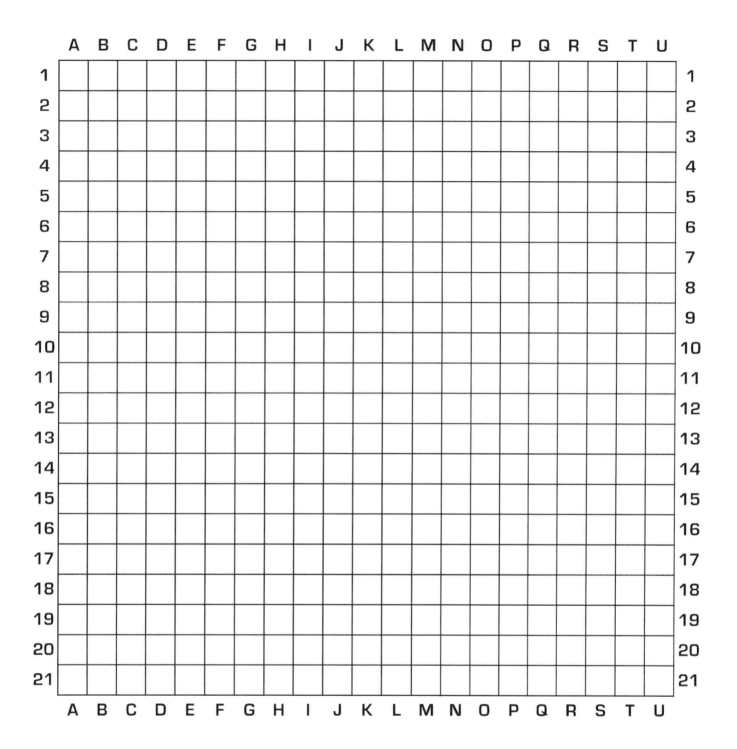

Clue: Chewy choices.

BRIGHT RED
2: I,J,K,L,M
3: H,I,J,K,L,M,N
14: H,I,M,N
15: H,I,M,N
16: H,I,M,N
17: G,H,I,M,N,O
18: G,H,I,M,N,O
19: G,H,N,O
20: F,G,N,O

DARK RED
18: J,K,L
19: I,M
20: I,M
21: E,F,G,H,I,J,K,L,M,N,O,P,Q

LIGHT GRAY or SILVER
14: J,K,L
15: J,L
16: J,L
17: J,K,L
19: J,L

BLACK
19: K
20: J,K,L

MAKE SOLID BLACK CIRCLES:
1: K
15: K
16: K

MAKE SOLID COLORED CIRCLES
Yellow
6: O
7: M,N
9: G,H,P
10: N
11: F,I
12: J,M
Green
8: M,O,P
9: K,O
10: K
11: H
12: K,O
13: I,J
Orange
7: O
8: L
9: J
10: G,M
11:P
12: H,N
13: L
Turquoise Blue
8: H
9: F,M
10: I,P
11: J,K
12: G
13: K,N

MAKE SOLID COLORED CIRCLES
Pink
7: P
8: J
9: I,L
11: G,N
12: I,L
Purple
8: G
10: H
11: L
13: H,M
Bright Red
8: N
10: F,J,O
11: M

CURVED BLACK OUTLINE
Draw a curved black line for glass bowl from:
Bottom right corner 3: G, to bottom left 6: F, down to bottom left 11: F & to bottom right 13: G. Repeat curved line on other side starting at bottom left corner 3: O to bottom right 6: P, down to 11: P, to bottom left 13: O.

DESIGN IDEA:
You can add the money symbol: 1¢ at the top of the bowl for fun.

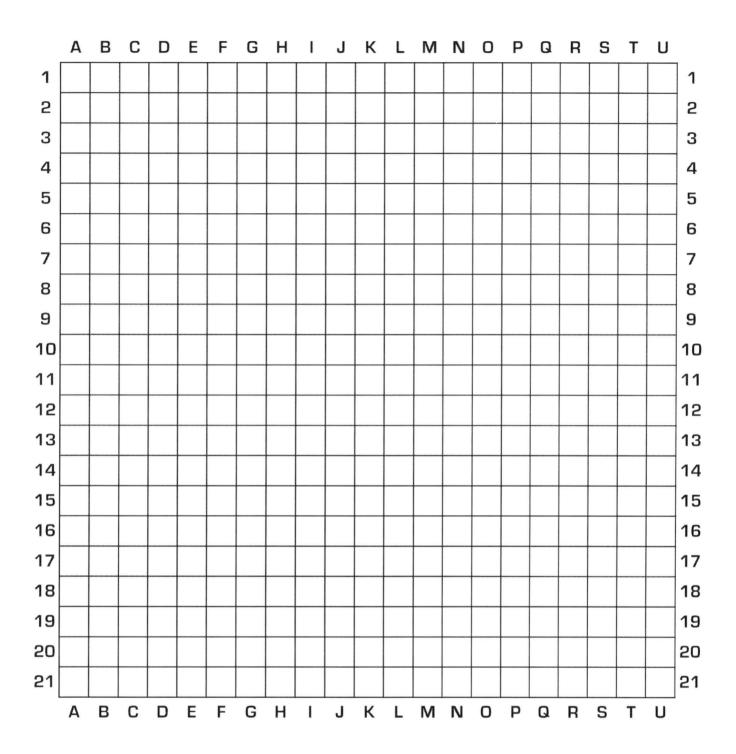

Clue: I scream, you scream, we all scream for this.

LIGHT BROWN or TAN
10: S,T
11: P,Q,R,S,T
12: N,O,P,Q,R,S,T
13: N,O,P,Q,R,S,T
14: O,P,Q,R,S,T
15: P,Q,R,S,T
16: Q,R,S,T
17: R,S,T
18: S,T

BROWN
5: E,F,G
6: D,G,Q,R
7: C,H,N,O,P,Q,R,S
8: B,C,D,E,F,G,H,I,M,N,O,P,Q,T
9: B,C,F,G,I,L,M,N,O,P
10: B,G,L,M
11: I,L
12: I
13: I
14: L
15: I
16: L
18: I
20: I,J,L
21: F,G,H,L

LIGHT OR LIME GREEN
5: N,O,P,Q,R
6: L,M,N,O,P,S
7: L,M
8: L
9: K
10: K
15: K
17: K
20: K
21: I,J,K

GRAY
9: D,E,H
10: C,D,E,F,H,I
11: B,C,D,E,F,G,H
12: C,D,E,F,G,H
13: D,E,F,G
14: D,E,F,G
15: E,F
16: E,F
17: D,E,F,G
18: C,D,E,F,G,H

PINK
3: M,N
4: L,M,N,O,P,Q
5: L,M
6: K
7: K
8: R,S
9: Q,R,S,T
10: N,O,P,Q,R
11: M,N,O
12: M
13: M
15: M
16: M
18: M
20: M
21: M,N,O

RED
Make a solid circle:
4: F
You can also add a green stem.

MULTI-COLORED DOTS
For fun, scatter colored dots all over the top of the pink.

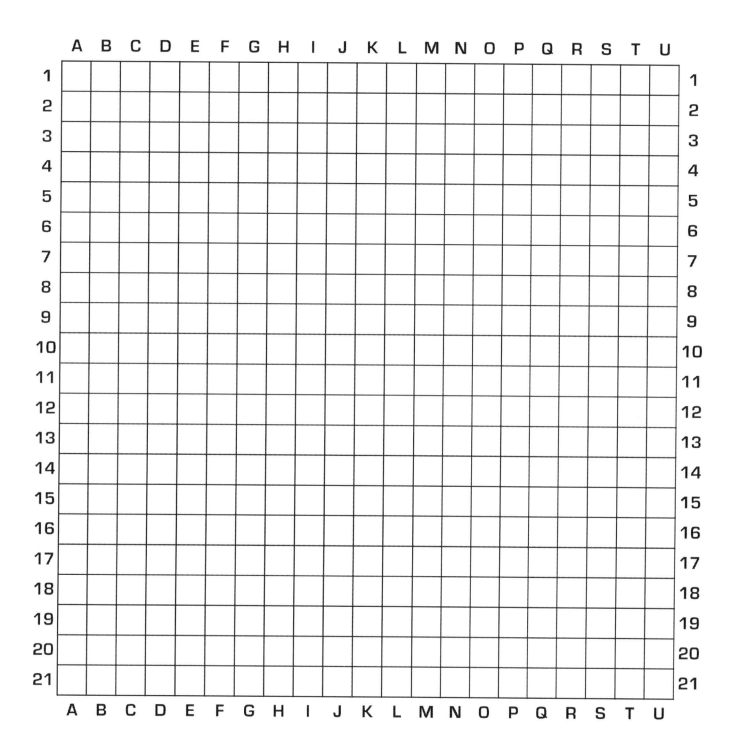

GRID 9

Clue: Just one short of a circus around here.

ORANGE
5: F,Q
6: A,C,E,Q,S
7: B,D,E,F,G,O,P,Q,R,T
8: C,D,E,Q,R,S
9: A,B,C,D,R,S,T
10: B,C,D,R,S,T,U

GOLDEN YELLOW
7: H,I,J,K,L,M,N
8: F,G,J,K,L,O,P
9: E,K,Q
10: E,Q

TAN or LIGHT BROWN
8: H,I,M,N
9: F,G,H,I,J,L,M,N,O,P
10: F,G,J,K,L,O,P
11: C,D,E,F,K,P,Q,R,S
12: B,E,Q,T
13: B,T
14: B,C,D,R,S,T

GREEN
3: O,P
4: N

BLUE
Make circles:
12: H and N

BLACK OUTLINE
Draw a curved black line from:
Lower left corner at 15: G
Curving down to:
Mid bottom line: 17: J, to
Mid bottom line: 17: L
Curving up to:
Lower right corner at 15: O

DARK GRAY
14: E,F,G,O,P,Q
15: E,F,G,H,N,O,P,Q
16: E,F,G,H,I,M,N,O,P,Q
17: F,G,H,I,J,K,L,M,N,O,P
18: G,H,I,J,K,L,M,N,O
19: H,I,J,K,L,M

RED
13: J,K,L
14: I,J,K,L,M
15: I,J,K,L,M
16: J,K,L

TURQUOISE BLUE
19: G,N
20: F,G,H,I,J,K,L,M,N,O
21: G,H,I,L,M,N
For blue hatband, highlight black line between 5 and 6 using 5 spaces from letter "I" through "M."

BLACK
4: I,J,K,L,M
5: I,J,K,L,M
6: G,H,I,J,K,L,M,N,O

PINK
Make circles:
1: R
2: Q,S
3: R

Fill in squares with pink:
12: C,D,R,S
13: C,D,R,S

DEEP PINK
Make a circle:
2: R

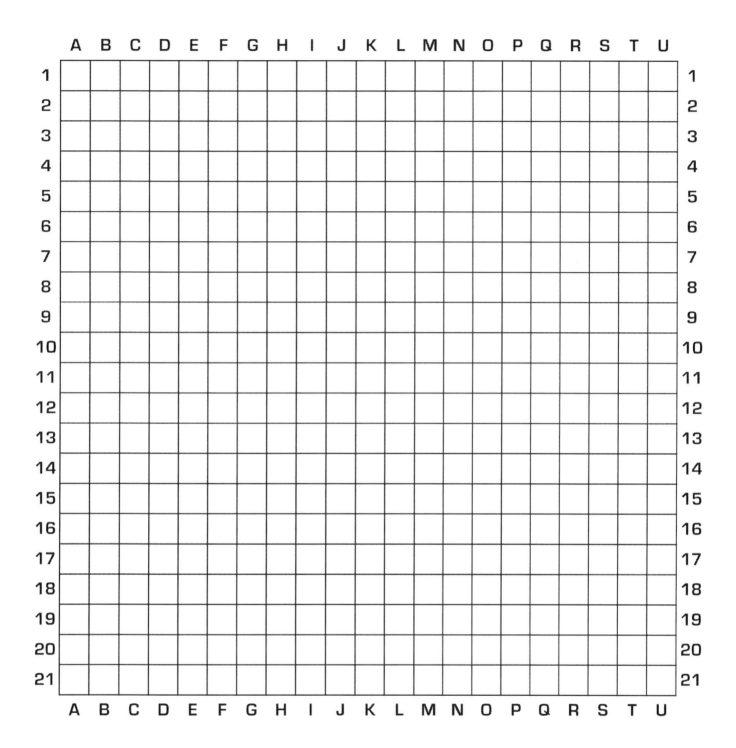

GRID 10

Clue: Sleeping in this bed could hurt.

PINK
2: D,E,F
3: D,E,F
4: D,E,F,K
5: J,K,L
6: B,I,J,K,O,P
7: B,C,D,I,J,K,Q
8: B,C,D,H,I,N,O,P,R
9: C,D,E,H,I,P,R
10: H,I,J,O,Q,R
11: H,I,J,L,M,N,P,Q
12: J,K,L,O,P,Q
13: E,F,G,K,L,M,N,O,P,Q
14: E,F,G,H,M,N,O
15: G,H
16: M,N
17: M,N,O,P
18: K,O,P
19: L,M,N

GREEN
1: I
2: J,N,O,P,Q
3: J,P
11: A
13: B
16: D,E
17: R,S
18: H,R
19: I,J
20: I

LIGHT GREEN
2: H,I
3: I,M,N,O
4: I,M,N,O
5: N
10: C
11: B
12: B
15: E,F
16: G,Q,R
17: J
18: I,J
19: K

DARK PINK
2: G
3: C,G,H
4: G,H,J,L
5: D,E,F,G,H,I,M,O,P
6: C,D,E,H,N,Q
7: E,G,H,P
8: E,Q
9: G,Q
11: R
12: D,E,F,G,R
13: H,J
14: I,J
15: I,J,K,L,M
16: H,I,J,K,L
17: K,L
18: L,M,N

MEDIUM RED
6: F,G
7: F,M,N
8: F,G,L,M,S
9: F,L,M,N,O,S,T
10: D,E,F,G,M,N,S,T
11: C,D,E,F,G,S,T
12: C,H,I,S,T
13: C,D,I,R,S,T
14: D,K,L,P,Q,R,S
15: D,N,O,P,Q,R
16: F,O,P
17: G,H,I,Q
18: Q
19: P

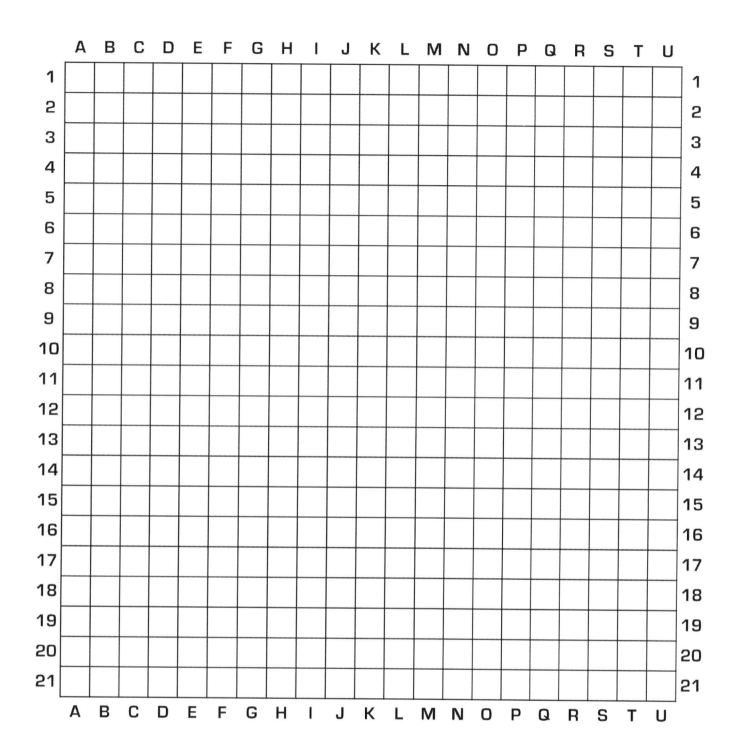

GRID 11

Clue: Bugs, Thumper and Energizer are cousins.

DARK GRAY
1: H,I,J,K
2: D,E,F,G,H,L
3: C,M
4: B,G,N
5: B,F,N
6: B,D,E,G,N
7: B,D,G,H,N
8: C,H,L,M
9: G,L
10: F,M
11: E,N,O
12: E,M,P
13: D,L,P
14: D,I,J,K,L,O
15: D,H,I,L,M,N
16: D,H,N
17: D,E,N
18: C,F,N
19: C,G,M
20: C,G,H,N
21: D,E,F,I,J,K,L,M,N,O

TURQUOISE BLUE
Make a solid circle:
5: K

PINK
4: D,E
5: D
Make a solid circle for nose:
Between 5 and 6 in column: O

YELLOW
4: S
5: R,T
6: P,S
7: O,Q
8: P

GREEN
7: S
8: S
9: P,R
10: P,Q
11: P
14: P
15: P,Q
16: P,R
17: P,S

ORANGE
Make solid circles:
5: S
7: P

BLACK
Draw a thin curved diagonal line from upper left corner down to lower right:
7: M

Draw 3 straight thin lines from center of nose, under eye and above smile for whiskers:
6 and 7: I through N

BACKGROUND COLOR
(OPTIONAL)
Light Green:
Line 17 down: Fill in bottom of picture behind design for grass.

Turquoise Blue:
Line 16 up: Fill in remaining background behind design for sky.

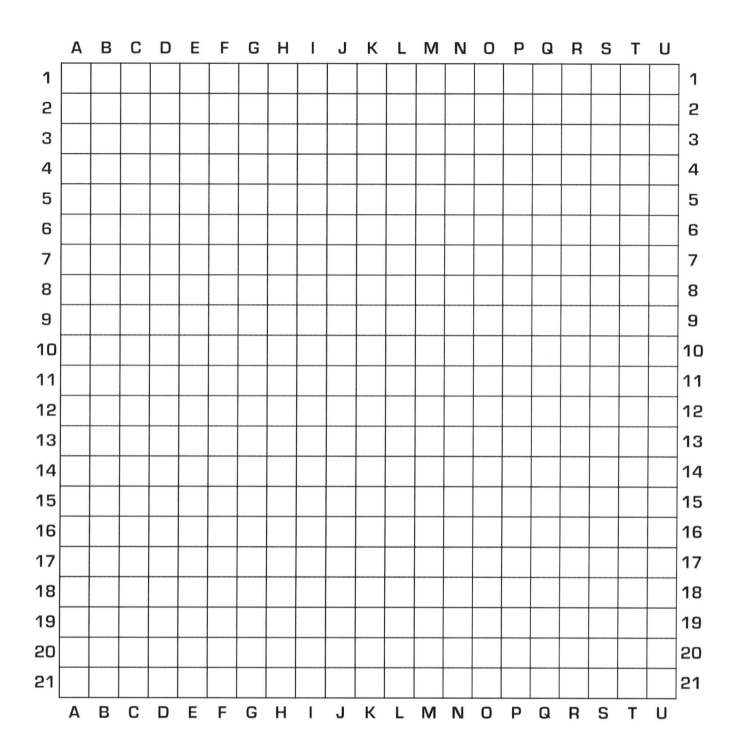

LORRAINE HOLNBACK BRODEK   43

GRID 12

Clue: Laundromutt.

BROWN:
5: J,K,L
6: I,M,N,Q,R,S
7: I,N,O,P,T
8: I,K,Q,T
9: I,K,Q,R,T
10: H,K,R,T
11: H,I,J,R,U
12: S,T,U
13: M,P
14: L,M,N,O,P
15: L,N,O,P,Q
16: K,M,N,O,P,Q
17: K,M,N,R,T,U
18: K,R,U
19: K,L,R,T,U
20: L,M,N,R,S,T
21: K,L,M,N,Q,R,S

GOLDEN TAN:
6: J,K,L
7: J,K,L,M,Q,R,S
8: J,L,M,N,O,P,R,S
9: J,L,M,P,S
10: I,J,L,Q,S
11: L,Q,S,T
12: M,P
13: N,O
15: M
16: L
17: L,O,P,Q
18: L,M,N,O,P,Q
19: M,N,O,P,Q
20: O,P,Q
21: O,P

RED:
7: D,E
8: C,D,E,F
9: B,C,D,E,F,G
10: C,D,E,F
11: C,D,E,F
12: C,D,E,F
13: B,C,D,E,F,G
14: B,C,F,G
15: B,C,F,G
16: C,D,E,F
17: C,D,E,F
18: C,D,E,F
19: C,D,E,F
20: B,C,D,E,F,G
21: B,C,D,E,F,G

GRAY:
13: A,H
14: A,D,E,H
15: D,E

BRIGHT BLUE:
Make solid blue circles:
1: J,K,L,M,N,O
2: H,I,L,N,P
3: G,H,L,O,Q
4: F,O,Q
5: E,O
6: D,E

BLACK:
Make solid black circles:
10: N,O

Draw two capital U's to fill
squares:
12: N,O

Draw smaller solid circle for nose
where top of U's meet at middle
of:
11 and 12: N and O

RED:
Draw straight red line for collar:
Between rows:
13 and 14: M through P

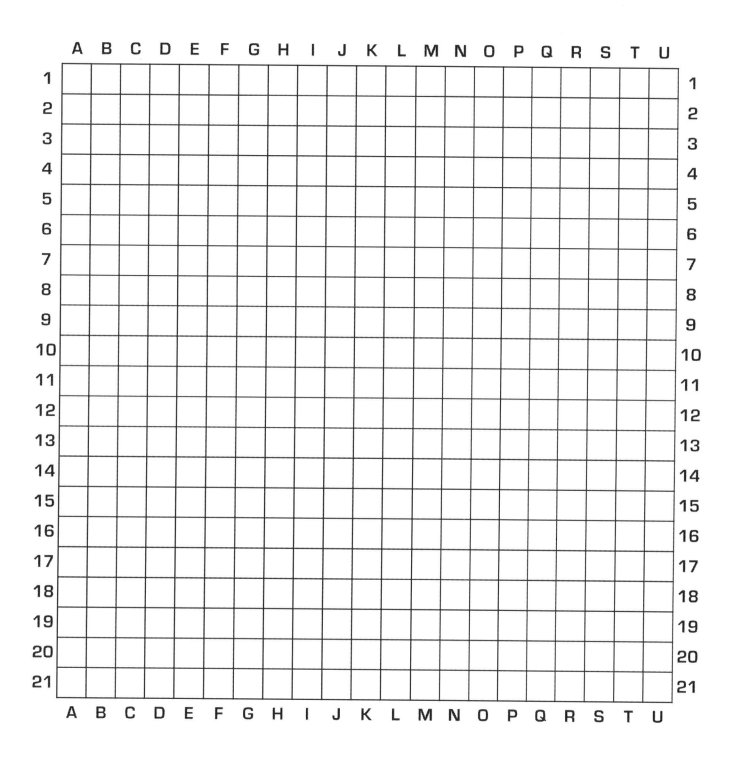

Clue: Have creek, will paddle.

BLUE
11: B,S
12: A,D,E,Q,R,T
15: B,E,R
16: A,C,D,F,H,J,M,O,Q,S
17: G,I,K,L,N,P
18: S
19: D,F,Q,R,T,U
20: C,E,G
Make a circle:
8: O

DARK ORANGE
9: P,Q

ORANGE
11: I
12: I,J
13: I,J,K,L,M,N
14: J,K,L,M,N,O
15: K,L,M,N

GOLDEN YELLOW
6: M,N,O
7: L,M,N,O,P
8: L,M,N,P
9: L,M,N,O
10: G,M,N,O
11: F,G,H,N,O,P
12: F,G,H,K,L,M,N,O,P
13: F,G,H,O,P
14: F,G,H,I,P
15: G,H,I,J,O
16: I,K,L,N

GREEN
7: A,F
8: B,E,S
9: B,C,D,T,U
10: C,D,U
11: C,U
12: C,U
13: C,U
14: C
15: C

BROWN
4: C
5: C,U
6: C,U
7: C,U
8: C,U
Make a short straight vertical line at top of each of brown cattail.

LIGHT BLUE
Fill in all remaining white squares from line 12 down through line 21.

LIGHT GRAY
1: B,C,D,E,L,M,N,O,P,Q,R,S,T,U
2: C,D,E,F,K,L,M,N,O,P,Q,R,S,T,U
3: L,M,N,R,S,T

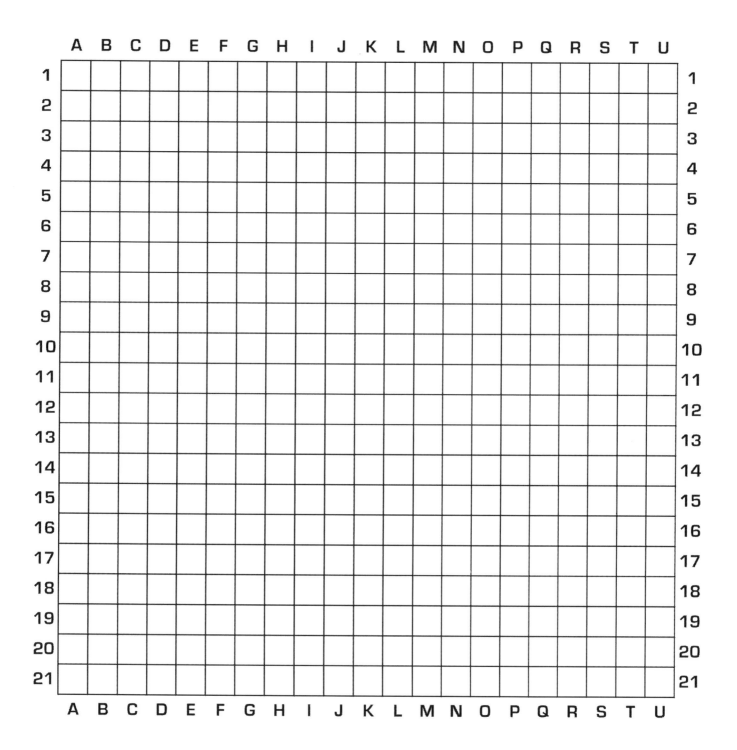

GRID 14

Clue: Upside down dessert.

GOLDEN YELLOW
9: H,L
10: G,K,O
11: F,H,J,L,N,P
12: E,G,I,K,M,O,Q
13: F,H,J,L,N,P
14: E,G,I,K,M,O,Q
15: F,H,J,L,N,P
16: E,G,I,K,M,O,Q
17: F,H,J,L,N,P
18: G,I,K,M,O
19: F,H,J,L,N
20: G,I,K,M
21: H,J,L

TAN or LIGHT BROWN
10: H,J,L,N
11: G,K,O
12: F,H,J,L,N,P
13: E,I,M,Q
14: F,H,J,L,N,P
15: G,K,O
16: F,H,J,L,N,P
17: E,I,M,Q
18: F,H,J,L,N,P
19: G,K,O
20: H,J,L,N
21: I,M

BROWN
Make solid circles:
9: K
11: M
13: G,K,O
15: E,I,M,Q
17: G,K,O
19: I,M
21: K

GREEN
Make solid circles:
1: K
2: J,K
3: J,K
4: J,K,O
5: F,G,J,K,N,O
6: G,J,K
7: G,H,J
8: G,H,I,L,M,N
9: E,F,G,I,J,M,N
10: I,M
11: I
You can outline edges with same
green or black color. Bring to a
point to make leaves; then fill in
with green.

LIGHT GREEN
Make solid circles:
2: H
3: H,N
4: H,I,M,N
5: H,I,L,M
6: H,I,L,M,N,O
7: I,K,L,M,N,O
8: J,K,O,
9: P
You can outline edges with same
light green or black. Bring to a
point to make leaves; then fill in
with light green. Some green
may overlap.

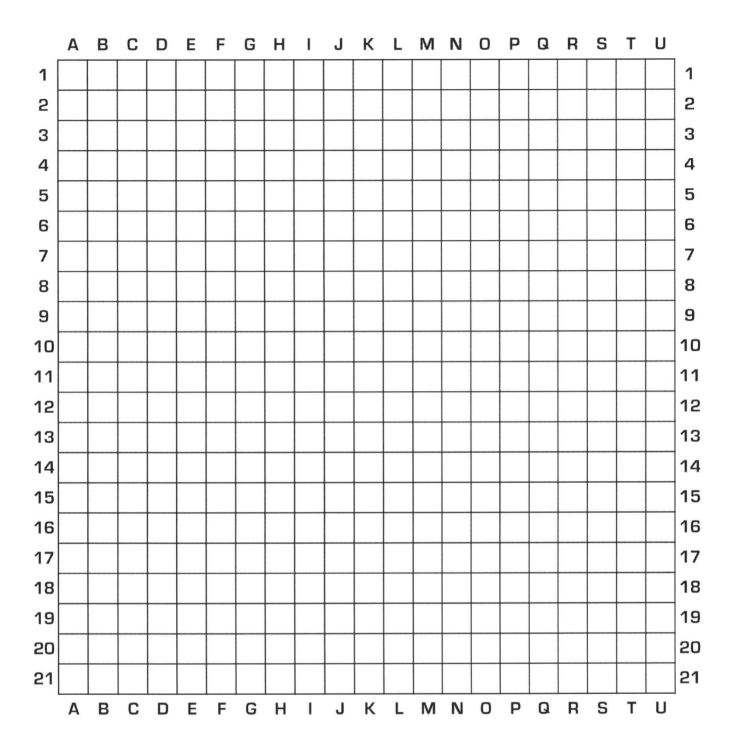

GRID 15

Clue: Mac Attack.

RED
2: B,D,F,H,J,L,N,P,R,T
4: B,D,F,P,R,T
6: B,D,R,T
8: B,D,T
10: B,T
12: B,T
14: B,T
16: B,D,F,R
18: B,D,F,H,J,L,N,P,R,T
20: B,D,F,H,J,L,N,P,R,T

LIGHT RED or PINK
1: B,D,F,H,J,L,N,P,R,T
2: A,C,E,G,I,K,M,O,Q,S,U
3: B,D,F,H,P,R,T
4: A,C,E,G,Q,S,U
5: B,D,F,R,T
6: A,C,S,U
7: B,D,T
8: A,C,S,U
9: B,T
10: A,C,U
11: B,T
12: A,C,U
13: B,T
14: A,C,U
15: B,D
16: A,C,E,S,U
17: B,D,F,H,J,L,N,P,R,T
18: A,C,E,G,I,K,M,O,Q,S,U
19: B,F,L,P,R,T
20: A,C,E,G,I,K,M,O,Q,S,U
21: B,D,F,H,J,L,N,P,R,T

TAN or LIGHT BROWN
4: I,J,K,L,M,N
5: H,I,J,K,L,M,N,O
6: G,H,I,J,K,L,M,N,O,P
7: F,G,H,I,J,K,L,M,N,O,P,Q
8: F,G,H,I,J,K,L,M,N,O,P,Q
14: F,H,I,M,O,Q
15: G,H,I,J,K,L,M,N,O,P

RED ORANGE
9: G,H,I,J,K,L,M,N,O,P

GOLDEN YELLOW
9: E,F,Q,R
10: F,G,H,I,J,K,L,M,N,O,P,R
11: I,J,K,L,M
12: K

DARK BROWN
10: E,Q
11: E,F,G,H,N,O,P,Q,R
12: E,F,G,H,I,J,L,M,N,O,P,Q,R
13: F,G,I,J,K,L,N,O,Q

LIGHT GREEN
13: D,H,M,P,R
14: E,K,N

GREEN
13: E,S
14: G,J,L,P,R

BLACK
Make solid black circles:
15: T
16: T
17: S
19: C,D,E,H,I,J,M,N,O

Draw thin black lines:
For each set of 3 solid black circles, draw 2 upside V's underneath, placing the tops of the V's on each side of the middle circle, for little ant legs like this:
^

Draw two pairs of legs for each ant, including the one turning the corner.
For fun, you can add tiny feet.
15 & 16: U
17: T
20: C,D,E,H,I,J,M,N,O

Draw a V on the top of each ant head for antennas. You can add tiny feelers too. Their heads are on the right:
14 & 15: S,T
19: E,F,J,K,O,P

Make tiny black dots:
Rows 4-8: If you want, scatter dots around the top of tan bun for sesame seeds.

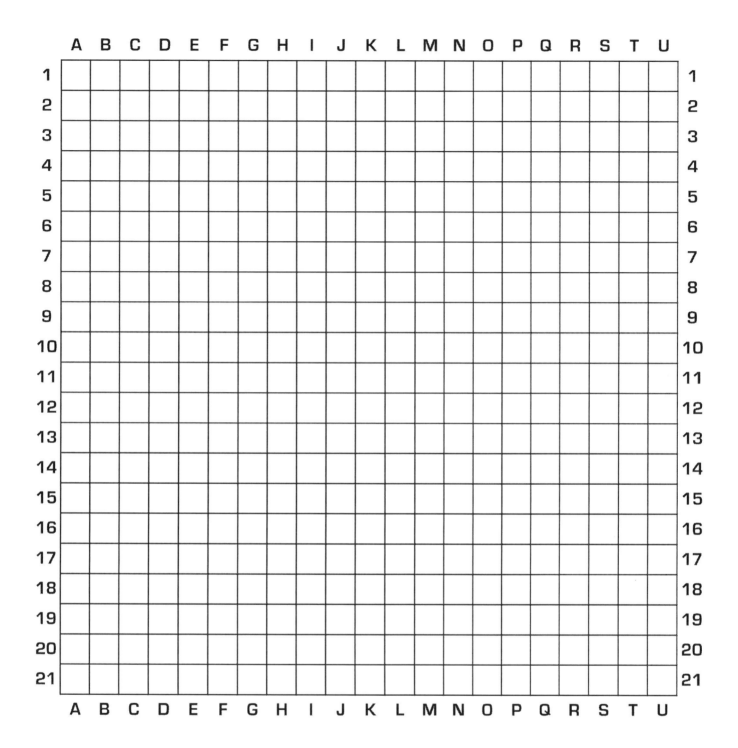

GRID 16

Clue: Hogwarts' messenger.

MEDIUM or RED BROWN
2: L,P
3: K,L,M,N,O,P
4: J,K,L,M,N,O,P,Q
5: I,J,K,L,N,O,P
6: I,J,K,O
7: I,J,K,O
8: J,K
9: K,L,N,P
10: K,L,M,Q
11: J,K,L,R
12: I,J,K,L,S
13: I,J,K,L,S
14: I,J,K,L,S
15: J,K,L,S
16: J,K
17: J,K
18: J,L,M,N,O
19: L,M,N
20: L

LIGHT OR GOLDEN BROWN
10: N,O,P
11: M,N,O,P,Q
12: M,N,O,P,Q,R
13: M,N,O,P,Q,R
14: M,N,O,P,Q,R
15: M,N,O,P,Q,R
16: O,P,Q

DARK BROWN
15: E,F
16: G,H,I,L,M,N,R,S
17: I,L,M,N,O,P,Q,R

GREEN
15: C,D
16: E
17: B,C,G,S
18: F,G,I,Q,T
19: E,T,U

LIGHT or OLIVE GREEN
16: C,D
17: H,T
18: E,R
19: H,S

BLACK
Draw curved diagonal lines for claws over branch from upper left corner down to lower right in squares:
17: O and Q

Make solid black circles. Leave a little white dot in center of each eye:
7: M,Q

Make solid circles for beak:
8: O
9: O

BLACK
Draw black outlines around eyes:
From top center of: 5: M
Diagonally down to lower left: 6: L
Straight down to lower left: 8: L
Diagonally down to center of: 9: M
Diagonally up to lower right: 8: N
Straight up to lower right: 6: N
Diagonally back up to meet: 5: M

Repeat this same outline design for other eye beginning at top center:
5: Q
Diagonally down to lower left: 6: P,
etc.

GOLDEN YELLOW
2: F,G,H,I
3: E,F,G,H,I,J
4: D,E,F,G,H,I
5: D,E,F,G,H
6: D,E,F,G,H
7: D,E,F,G,H
8: E,F,G,H,I
9: F,G,H,I
Draw a circle outline around yellow squares with yellow or black.

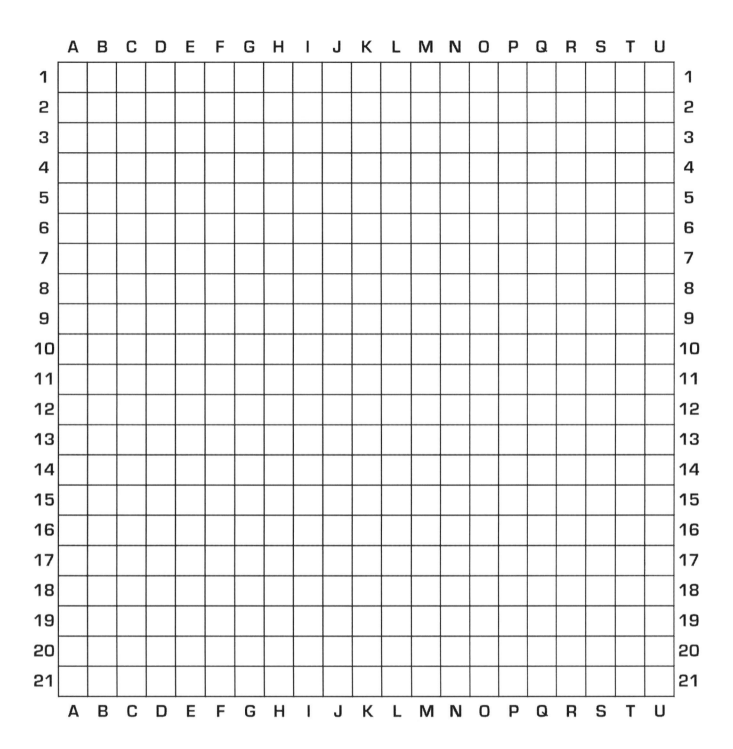

GRID 17

Clue: The hit of the fiesta.

BRIGHT PINK
4: B,C
5: C
6: D,S
7: S
8: R
9: Q
10: P
12: F,G,H,I,J,K,L,M,N,O,P,Q
17: B,T
18: C,S
19: G,Q
20: F,P

GREEN
1: H
2: I,J
3: D,K,Q
4: D,E,R
5: D,E,F,Q
6: E,F
13: F,G,H,I,J,K,L,M,N,O,P,Q

ORANGE
7: D,E
8: C,E,T,U
9: A,B,D,E,F,S,T
10: A,B,C,E,F,R
11: B,Q
16: D,E,P,Q,R
17: F,G,O,P

PURPLE
7: F
8: F,G
9: G,H
10: G,I,J,L,M,N,O
11: H,I,J,K,L,M,N,O,P
16: C,S
17: C,D,R,S
18: F,G,O,P
19: E,F,O,P

TURQUOISE BLUE
9: C
10: D,H,K
11: C,E,F,G
14: E,F,G,H,I,M,N,O,P,Q

YELLOW
6: U
7: T
8: S
9: R
10: Q
15: D,E,F,G,H,N,O,P,Q,R
16: F,G,N,O

MEDIUM BROWN
1: R,S,T,U
2: P,Q,R
3: L,M,N,O,P

LIGHT GREEN
2: K
3: J
4: Q
5: P
6: P

MAKE SOLID CIRCLES OF COLOR:
Black
8:D
Bright Pink
15: K
Green
19: L
21: K
Orange
19: K
Turquoise Blue
17: K
20: J
Yellow
18: J
21: L

DRAW A THICK LINE FOR STRING:
Turquoise
Make a curved line down from the top center of the tree branch at:
Top of 3: N
Curved down to: 7: L
Then straight down to bottom of: 9: K

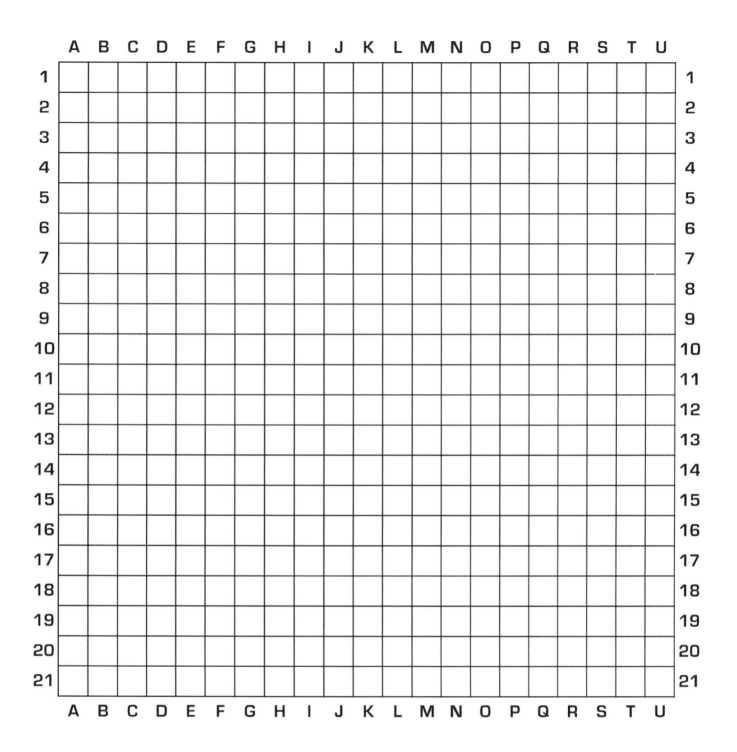

GRID 18

Clue: Hanging out at the zoo.

DARK BROWN
2: J,K,M,N
3: I,J,K,L,M,N,O
4: H,I,K,L,M,O,P
5: G,H,P,Q
6: G,H,P,Q
7: H,I,O,P
8: I, O
11: B,C,D
12: A,C,D,E
13: A,E,F,G,H,I,J,K,L,M,N,O
14: F,G,H,I,O,P,Q,R
15: H,P,Q,R,S
16: H,P,R,S
17: H,I,O,P,Q,R
18: H,I,J,K,L,M,N,O,P
19: I,J,K,L,M,N,O

BLACK OUTLINE:
Draw thick black line for smile from:
Upper left corner: 10: I, down to:
Lower right corner: 11: J, across to:
Lower right corner: 11: M, up to:
Upper right corner : 10: O

PINK
4: F,G,Q,R
5: E,F,R,S
6: E,F,R,S
7: F,R
19: H,P
20: H,I,J,N,O,P

Make a solid pink circle: 16: L

LIGHT or GOLDEN BROWN
2: F,G,Q,R
3: E,F,G,H,P,Q,R,S
4: D,E,S,T
5: D,T
6: D,T
7: E,G,Q,S
8: F,G,J,K,L,M,N,Q,R
9: I,J,K,L,M,N,O
10: H,I,J,K,L,M,N,O,P
11: H,I,J,K,L,M,N,O,P
12: J,K,L,M,N
14: J,K,L,M,N
15: I,J,K,L,M,N,O
16: I,J,K,M,N,O
17: J,K,L,M,N

BLACK
Make solid circles:
5: J,N
7: L

GREEN
14: A,B
15: C

GOLDEN YELLOW
Make solid yellow circles:
15: B
16: C,D
17: C,D,E
18: B,D,E
19: A,C,E
20: D

BLACK OUTLINE
Draw a curved black line for tail:
Starting at middle of: 8: U
Make a curve up under ear at: 7: T,U
Continue curving down to: 11: U
Ending at lower left corner: 14: S
Now highlight tail in dark brown.

To accent 3 bananas, you can outline edges with yellow or black. Bring to a rounded point; then fill in with color.

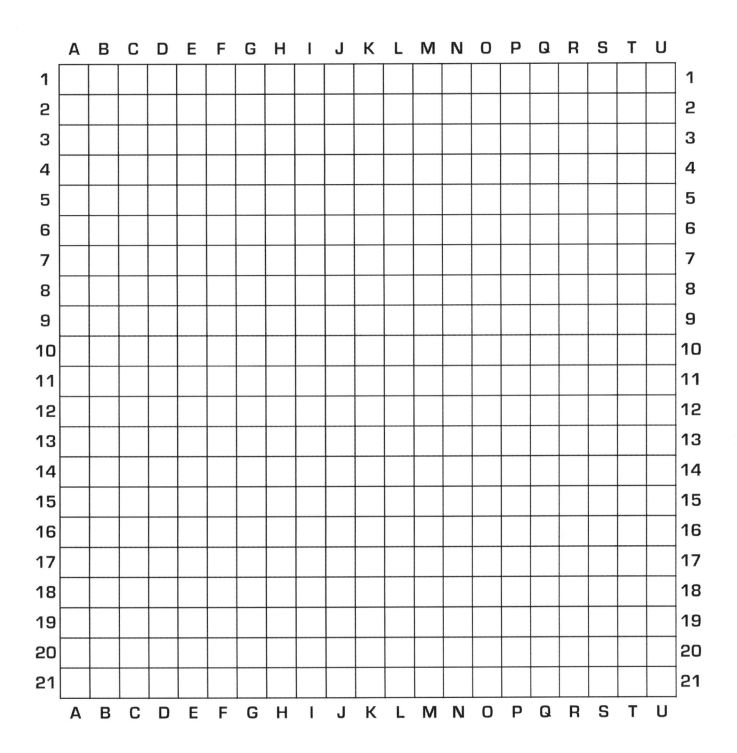

GRID 19

Clue: They love to hang out in schools.

GREEN
11: K
12: A,J
13: B,J,Q,U
14: B,J,Q,T
15: B,J,Q,S
16: B,H,Q,T
17: A,P,U
18: A,H,O,U
19: I,T
20: A,G,H,O,T
21: B,I,P,T

LIGHT GREEN
14: K
15: K,R
16: R
17: H,Q,T
18: B,P,T
19: B,H,P,U
21: H,O,S

RED ORANGE or CORAL
14: A
15: A
16: A,D
17: B,D,F
18: C,D,F,Q,S
19: A,D,E,F,N,O,Q,S
20: B,C,P,Q,R
21: D,Q

GOLDEN YELLOW
7: N,P
8: M,O,Q
9: N,P,R
10: O,Q
13: L
14: H,L,N
15: I,L,M,O
16: I,J,K,L,O
17: L,N
18: J,L,M
19: J,L,M
20: I,K,L
21: L

BLUE
1: D,E,F,G
2: A,C,D,F,H
3: A,B,C,E,G,I,J,K
4: A,B,D,F,G,H,I
5: A,C,E,F,G
6: D,E

ORANGE
6: N,O,P,Q
7: L,M,O,Q,R,S,U
8: K,N,P,R,S,T,U
9: K,L,M,O,Q,S,T,U
10: L,M,N,P,R,S,U
11: M,N,O,P,Q,R
12: N,O

PURPLE
2: E,G
3: D,F
4: C,E
5: D

PINK or LAVENDER
10: D,E,F
11: C,E,G
12: C,D,E,F,G

THIN BLACK LINES:
Starting from bottom of row 12, draw five vertical squiggly lines like dangling worms. Now, highlight these squiggly lines with pink or lavender:
Row C: 13-17
Row D: 13-15
Row E: 13-18
Row F: 13-16
Row G: 13-17

MAKE SOLID BLACK CIRCLES:
3: H
8: L
11: D,F

BLACK CIRCLE OUTLINES:
Fill in the squares with round black circles for air bubbles like this: O
1: K,O
2: M
3: O
4: M
5: L
6: G
7: C
8: E,G
9: C

LIGHT BLUE
Leaving air bubbles white, you may also fill in the background with light blue using varying pressure with your pencil, crayon or pen for shading effect.

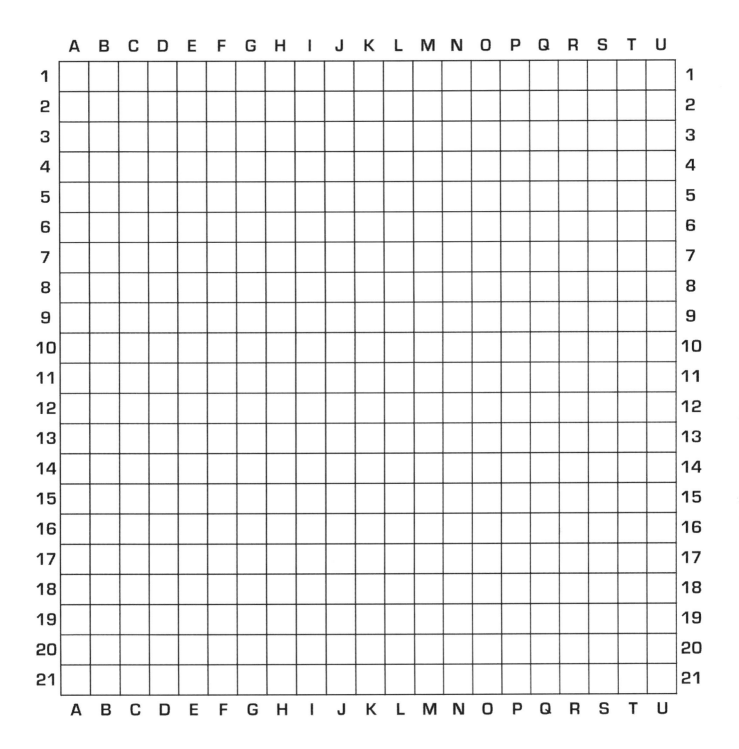

Clue: A really cool guy!

LIGHT BLUE
1: A,C,D,E,F,G,H,I,J,R,S,T,U
2: A,B,C,D,E,F,H,I,S,U
3: A,B,C,E,F,G,H,I,R,S,T,U
4: B,C,D,F,G,H,I,J,R,T,U
5: A,B,C,F,G,I,J,R,S,T,U
6: A,B,G,H,T,U
7: A,H,I,J,R,S,T,U
8: A,B,H,I,S,U
9: A,B,C,H,I,S,T,U
10: A,C,D,H,I,J,R,S,T
11: A,B,C,D,E,F,G,I,J,K,Q,R,T,U
12: A,B,C,D,F,G,H,J,R,S,T,U
13: B,C,D,E,F,G,H,I,T,U
14: A,B,C,D,E,G,H,T
15: A,B,D,E,F,G,H,T,U
16: A,B,C,D,F,H,T
17: A,B,C,D,E,F,G,H,T,U
18: A,G,H,T,U
19: H,I,S,T

BLACK
2: K,L,O,Q
3: K,L,M,O,P,Q
4: K,L,M,N,O,P,Q
6: I,J,K,L,M,N,O,P,Q,R,S

Now make solid black circles:
8: M,O
14: N
19: N

RED
5: K,L,M,N,O,P,Q
11: L,M,N,O,P
12: P,Q
13: P,R,S
14: P

LIGHT YELLOW
4: E
5: D,E
6: C,D,E,F
7: A,B,C,D,E,G
8: C,D,F,G
9: E,F,G
10: E,F,G

MEDIUM BROWN
7: F
8: E
9: D
11: H
12: I
13: J
14: K
15: L
16: M
17: N
18: O
19: P
20: Q
21: R

GREEN
16: P
17: L,M,O,P
18: L

THIN BLACK OUTLINES:
Draw a curved line for smile (n white row above red scarf):
From upper left corner: 10: M
Down to bottom line: 10: N
Across and up to right corner: 10: O

Using slightly curved diagonal lines, outline both sides of brown stripe going across yellow broom: Between rows 7 and 9: D up to F

You can outline broom. Fill in with more yellow and brown to the lines.

Outline and round the edges of two separate green areas. Fill in with more green to the line.

Draw a "V" on an angle for nose and then fill in with orange:
9: N

MORE OUTLINE IDEAS:
You can outline the snowy ground for a more solid effect.

For fun, you can draw pencil circles or *'s in the empty white spaces in blue background behind figure.

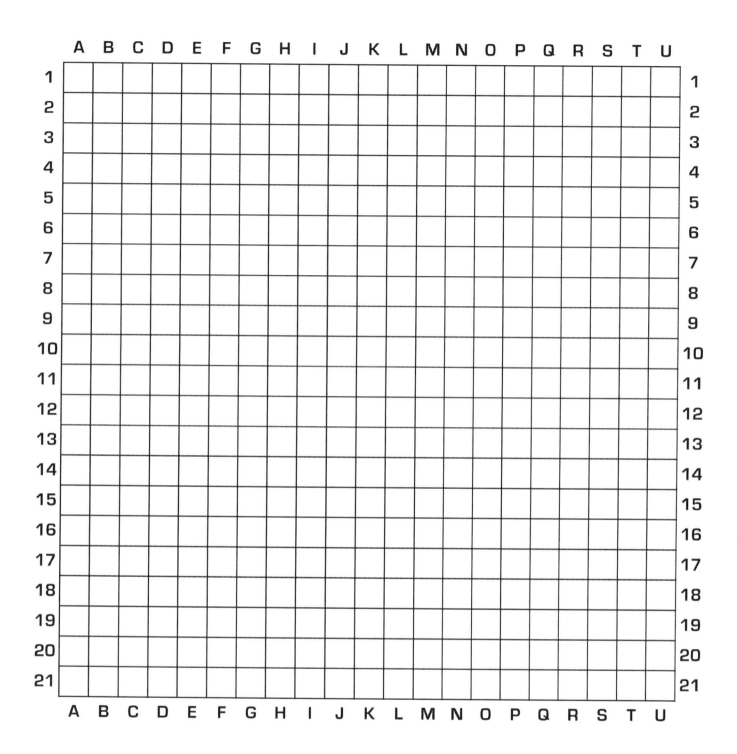

GRID 21

Clue: Peep Patrol.

RED
1: P,Q,R,S,T
2: O,Q,R,S,T,U
3: N,R,S,T,U
4: M,S,T,U

BROWN
2: P
3: O,Q
4: N,R
5: M,S
6: N,R
7: O,P,Q,R,S,T,U
9: R,S
10: R,S
12: R,S
13: R,S
14: R,S
15: R,S
16: R,S
18: R,S
19: R,S
20: R,S
21: R.S

GOLDEN YELLOW
3: P
4: O,P,Q
5: N,O,Q,R,T,U
6: O,P,Q,S,T,U

GREEN
8: Q,R,S,T
11: O,P,Q,R,S,T,U
17: P,Q,R,S,T,U

BLACK
Make a solid black circle:
5: P

Now draw a slanted straight line down from the black circle outwards: about 3 squares long for landing stick:
Between rows 5 and 6: M through P

PINK
6: D,E,J,K
7: D,K
20: G,H,J

TAN
6: F,G,H,I
7: E,F,G,H,I,J
8: D,E,F,I,J,K
9: D,E,J,K
10: D,E,F,I,J,K
11: E,F,G,H,I,J
12: A,B,F,G,H,I
13: B,E,G,H
14: A,D,F,G,H,I
15: A,C,E,G,H
16: A,D,F
17: A,C,E,G,H,J
18: A,D,G,H,J
19: A,G,H,J
20: A,B,C

LIGHT TAN
13: F,I
14: E,J
15: D,F,I,J
16: C,E,G,H,I,J
17: B,D,F,I
18: B,C,E,F,I
19: B,C,D,E,F,I
20: D,E

DARK GREEN
19: P
20: F,M,P,U
21: A,C,F,G,I,K,L,M,P,Q

LIGHT or YELLOW GREEN
19: L,N,U
20: I,K,O,T
21: B,D,E,H,J,N,O,T,U

BLACK
Draw a black circle for nose: at intersection of: G and H: 9 and 10

Draw two capital U's for mouth under nose touching black circle in the middle:
10: G,H

BLACK
Draw two black circles for eyes: on line between rows 8 and 9: at: intersections of F and G and H and I

Draw three straight thin lines from top of left and right side of mouth for whiskers:
Rows: 9 and 10
Make them at different angles and lengths. Use four squares at the longest:
8 and 11: C through F
8 and 11: I through L

Make thin curved outlines for ears if you would like to make them more pointy.
6: D,E,J,K
7: D,K

TURQUOISE BLUE
Make solid blue circles:
4: H
5: H
9: O
10: O
15: T
16: T

BLACK
Make tiny black circles on top blue circles for eyes:
4: H
9: O
15: T

Make tiny left arrowheads: < for beaks and tails:
4: I
10: P
15: U

Make tiny right arrowheads: > for beaks and tails:
5: G
9: N
16: S

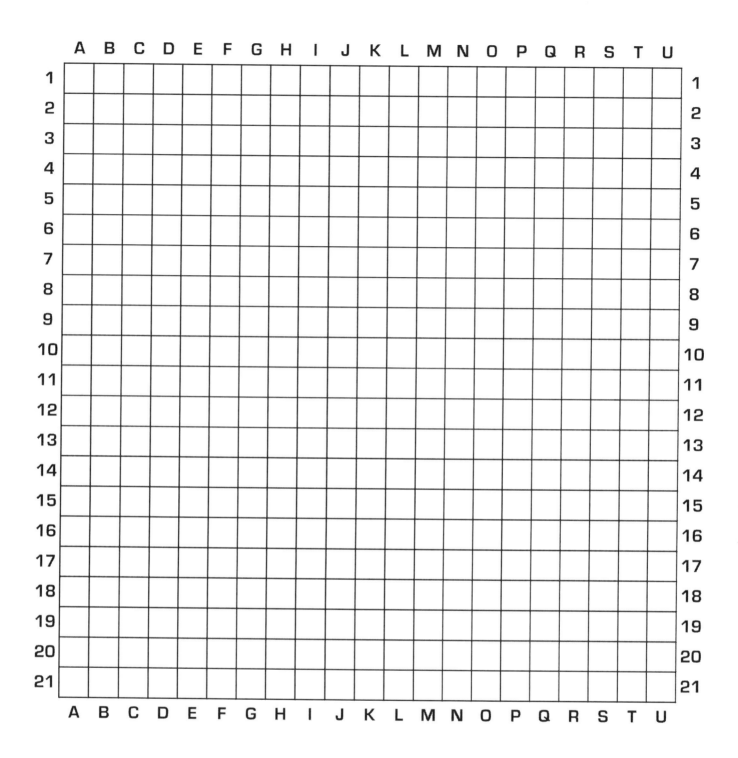

Clue: Crop Cop.

BROWN
1: J,K,L
3: G,H,I,J,K,L,M,N,O
8: A,B,C,S,T,U
17: K
18: K
19: K
20: K
21: K

RED
8: D,F,H,K,N,P,R
9: E,G,O,Q
10: D,F,H,K,N,P,R

PALE RED or LIGHT PINK
8: E,G,O,Q
9: D,F,H,K,N,P,R
10: E,G,O,Q

TAN
4: I,K,M
5: I,J,L,M
6: I,J,K,L,M
7: J,K,L

GOLDEN YELLOW
4: H,N,
5: H,N
7: C,S
9: C,S
20: H,I,M,N

BLUE or DENIM BLUE
8: I,J,L,M
9: I,J,L,M
10: I,J,L,M
11: H,J,K,L,N
12: H,I,J,K,L
13: H,I,J,K,L,M
14: H,I,K,L,M,N
15: H,K,L,M,N
16: H,I,J,K,L,M,N
17: H,I,J,L,M,N
18: H,I,M,N
19: H,I,M,N

PURPLE
14: J
15: I,J

ORANGE
2: J,K,L
12: M,N
13: N
17: P,S
18: C,E,O,P,Q,R,S,T
19: B,C,D,E,F,O,P,Q,R,S,T
20: B,C,D,E,F,O,P,Q,R,S,T
21: C,D,E,P,Q,R,S

GREEN
15: R
16: C,Q
17: D,Q,R
18: D

BLACK
MAKE SOLID BLACK CIRCLES:
4: J,L
5: F (leave little white dot in middle)
6: F
11: I,M

DRAW THIN BLACK LINES:
For smile, starting at lower left:
5: J
Draw a line down to center bottom 6: K
Curving line back up to lower right:
5: L

For beak, make one short horizontal line like this: –
5:G

For tail, make one right arrowhead like this: >
6:E

For legs, make two vertical thin lines down:
7: F

For straw effect, make three thin black lines coming out of face, arms & pants on top of all yellow squares.

Draw a "V" on an angle for nose and then fill in with dark orange:
5: K

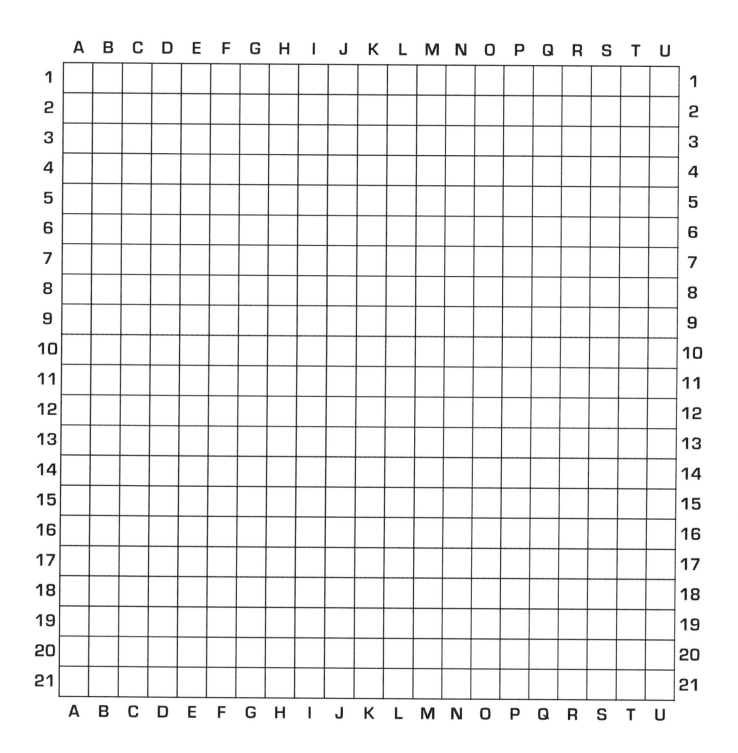

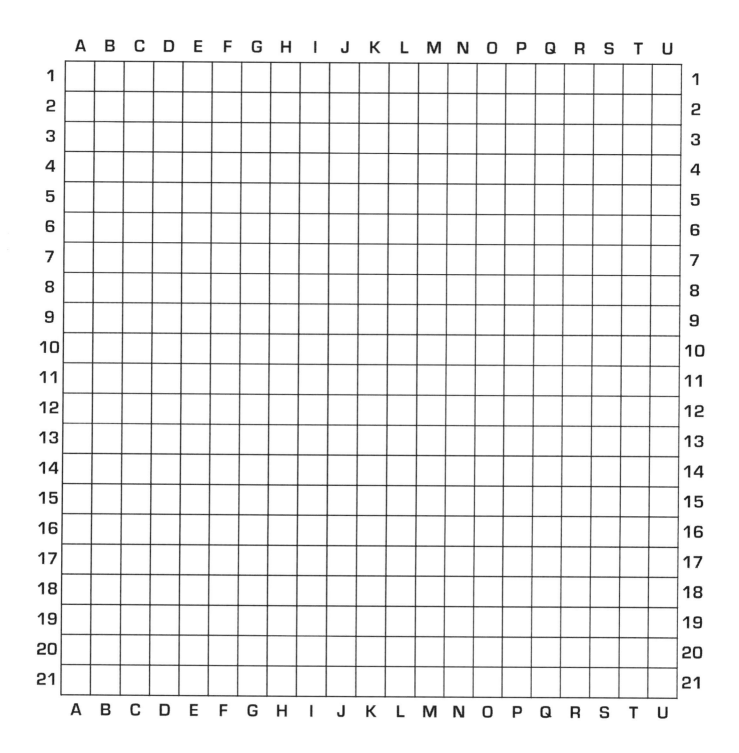

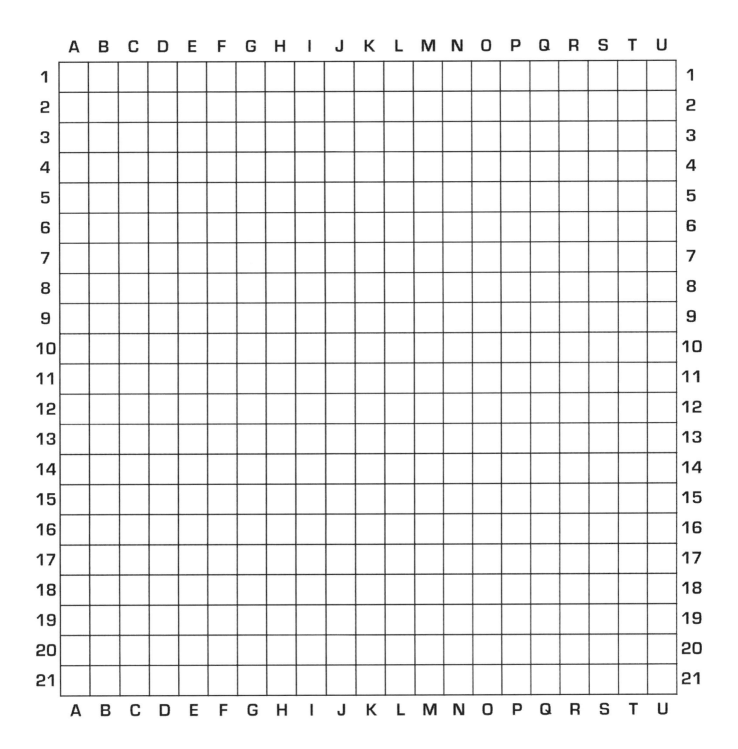

SOLUTIONS

SOLUTIONS

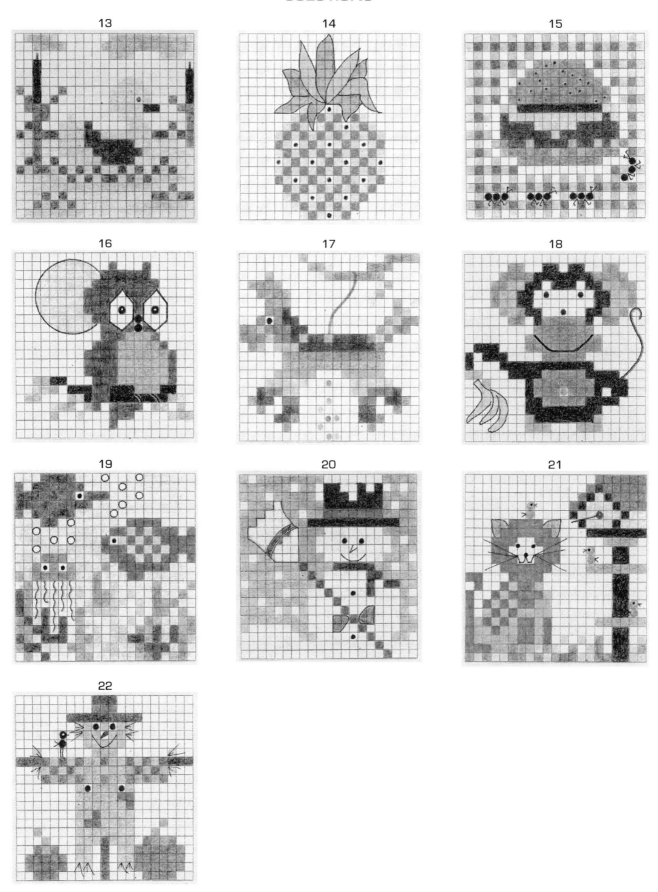

Cut out, then trace or paste onto heavy paper. Cut out this thicker template and use it as your line guide.

Made in the USA
Lexington, KY
02 July 2016